# MASTERING MOTIVATION !

## Forthcoming titles in this series will include

- *Winning Sales Letters*
- *Win–Win Negotiation*
- *How to Wow an Audience*
- *Make the Most of Meetings*
- *Key Account Management*
- *Coping with Company Politics*
- *Winning CVs*
- *How to Pay Less Tax*

*Do you have ideas for subjects which could be included in this exciting and innovative series? Could your company benefit from close involvement with a forthcoming title?*

Please contact David Grant Publishing Limited
80 Ridgeway, Pembury, Tunbridge Wells, Kent TN2 4EZ
Tel/Fax +44 (0)1892 822886
Email GRANTPUB@aol.com
with your ideas or suggestions.

# MASTERING

# MOTIVATION

**!**

## John Frazer-Robinson

# 60 Minutes Success Skills Series

First published 1999 by
David Grant Publishing Limited
80 Ridgeway
Pembury
Kent TN2 4EZ
United Kingdom
Tel/Fax +44 (0)1892 822886
Email GRANTPUB@aol.com

01   00   99          10 9 8 7 6 5 4 3 2 1

60 Minutes Success Skills Series is an imprint of
David Grant Publishing Limited

*British Library Cataloguing in Publication Data*
A CIP catalogue record for this book is available from the British Library

ISBN 1-901306-28-3

*Cover design: Liz Rowe*
*Text design: Graham Rich*
*Production coordinator: Paul Stringer*
*Edited and Typeset in Futura by Kate Williams*
*Printed and bound in Great Britain by*
*T.J. International Ltd, Padstow, Cornwall*

*This book is printed on acid-free paper*

# CONTENTS

### ABOUT *MASTERING MOTIVATION*

Was your most recent day at work a good one? Did you get things done – achieve? Did you have some fun? Did you build in a little quality time with other people? Did you come home feeling good and looking forward to tomorrow? Your motivation is high!

If you had a bad day and are not looking forward to tomorrow or the week ahead, then you have to do something about it. You have to rev up. This book will tell you how.

Motivated people get things done. They have energy, commitment, pride in what they do and they are far more likely to reach targets, goals or objectives. They achieve. They succeed.

Motivation is becoming increasingly vital for managers in today's business climate. People have to work hard for their money. There's lots of work to be done, and with the emphasis simultaneously, and paradoxically, on speed, quality and price, the pressure is on almost everywhere.

Most working people suffer from stress and pressure from time to time. The result can be loss of confidence, low morale and plummeting self-esteem. Whether that is true for you today as you read this book or whether it was true at some other time in your past or will be true in your future – knowing how to dig yourself out of it and overcome it, or to dig someone you manage out of it, is important.

### How does this book work?

Settle yourself somewhere quiet and comfortable and read the entire book. Next, use the book for reference – when you need some help, glance through it to remind yourself of all the various ideas and thoughts. Lastly, refresh your ideas by using the book on an ongoing basis. Why not re-read a different chapter each month?

## About the 60 Minutes Success Skills Series

The 60 Minutes Success Skills Series is written for people with neither the time nor the patience to trawl through acres of jargon, management-speak and page filling waffle. Like all books in the series, *Mastering Motivation* has been written in the belief that it is possible to learn all you really need to know quickly and without hassle. The aim is to distil the essentials and give practical advice that you can start to put into practice straight away.
Good luck!

## Coming up in this chapter

*Why we all respond to motivation*
*Motivation and management*
*Becoming a master of motivation*
*What do winners do?*

## Understanding yourself and your people

It is possible to increase your own motivation to a peak and maintain it there and to avoid any troughs when you have an understanding of what motivates you – as long as you use that understanding to avoid being trapped by negative thinking or apathy.

> " *It might sound a bit 'Californian' to others, but every morning I dress myself and put my make-up on to feel as good as it is possible to be. Then I stand in front of the mirror and admire myself. On the way to work I remind myself of all the things I have done well in the last few days and of all the wonderful opportunities held by the day ahead. Motivated? You bet!!* "
> **– Lynne Varley, Administration Manager, NHS Trust**

I have put off starting this book for over a week now, so I've had to motivate myself to do it. Interestingly, money is not a part of it – it's not just that the publisher is too mean (they all are!), but money is not actually a great motivator unless there is something wrong.

So what did I do to get myself going? I created motivation for myself. I changed the way I was feeling. How?

○ *By taking away my own excuses*
○ *By setting achievable goals*
○ *By recognising and valuing all the positive outcomes from completing the book*
○ *By making myself safe and comfortable with the task*
○ *By remembering all my achievements and successes as an author*

○ *By thinking about all the others who might benefit (like you, I hope!)*

As a result, when I came to sit at my keyboard, I felt highly motivated, positive and enthusiastic. Now I can't wait to share my ideas and experiences with you. And I know that in just 63 pages, I can give you all you need to master motivation for yourself and for those you manage or supervise. And the exercise of getting myself going provides the first thing to notice about motivation. Motivation is something we feel. It's about our feelings.

> I was working with a recently founded company in South Africa. After the big press launch I came across a group of three women in animated, excited conversation. I asked what was exciting them so much. One replied, 'We were just saying how great it is to work somewhere where you hate going home at night and you can't wait to get to the office in the morning'.

## What is motivation?

The dictionary definition of motivation is, 'The action or an act of motivating something or someone'. That's a bit obvious, but it does go on to be a little more helpful: 'The conscious or unconscious stimulus, incentive or motive, etc. for action towards a goal especially as resulting from psychological or social factors; the factors giving purpose or direction to the behaviour'. That's a little nearer what we need, but for the purpose of this book I think we'll write our own definition. Motivation is getting people, cheerfully, willingly and professionally, to do the things that the business requires them to do.

So now let's notice a second thing about motivation. It can be achieved in two ways: formally and environmentally. That is to say, there are things you can do about motivation – exercises, teamwork, games and so on – which build motivation, but the working environment you create also affects motivation. If you create conditions where coming to work feels good, and where people get things done, celebrate their achievements, learn, grow and develop from things that go wrong – then they enjoy themselves. They feel fulfilled by their work. They work in a positive, exciting, effective place. Motivation builds naturally and is accelerated by your formal motivation work. You're not trying to get water to flow uphill. The energy of yourself and your team is working in glorious harmony. Everybody is happy.

## Above all, a manager cares

Creating motivation is a vital task of management. It contributes greatly to your own motivation, and when you are surrounded by buzzing, energetic, excited individuals it's catching! This is especially so when you know you have played a major part in developing that spirit. My advice is that the responsibility for motivation should be recognised formally in a manager's job specification.

Leadership today is about recognising just how much of the management task lies in mentor and motivator roles. And it's also about realising how very, very little lies in telling people what to do. Instead of telling people what to do, you help them to know what to do. You help them to acknowledge and understand their own successes and failures. You help them to find their true potential. You support, counsel, encourage, demonstrate and coach. There's an emotional and psychological content to your work. All of this builds motivation.

Your team culture should see ignorance as the opportunity to learn and failure as an opportunity to succeed. Your culture should welcome those who say, 'Tell me more. I'd like to learn that.' Make no mistake, businesses cannot tolerate ignorance and failure. Life is too tough, too competitive, to carry those who don't, or won't, learn.

> As a manager your task is to cultivate and motivate your team. Your manager's task is to cultivate and motivate you, but you must demonstrably join in and take initiatives. Make sure that your manager is paying enough attention to your motivation. If you don't feel you are receiving enough attention – SHOUT. And shout loudly. If your manager doesn't respond, don't give up! Find a peer and work together to support each other.

### Stars in their eyes

Nowadays senior management is looking for enterprise and initiative from its stars. It is in assisting your team to meet their personal needs and the needs of the business that you and your management can best achieve success.

Your task is to develop your team to enable them to coast to their targets, objectives and goals, knowing that you are constantly supporting them, improving their skills, fine tuning their knowledge and capabilities, and helping them to succeed in a changing and competitive environment.

That will feel like real management. It demonstrates trust in them and care for them. It enables them to do their job with confidence and capability. It benefits all concerned. This is the approach of someone who understands motivation and realises that if they develop their people, both they and their team move nearer their personal and corporate objectives. This is how to manage a team destined for success. Every day yields improvement. Every week offers growth and development. Every month leads to a better chance of success. Every year is a positive and powerful period for you and your team because you are a buzzing, exciting, energetic and motivational manager – the best kind to be.

### What turns YOU on?

Get to know yourself as a manager. Write down a description of yourself. One paragraph will do. List your personal strengths and weaknesses. Then do a paragraph for each of your team members too. Examine why you get on better with some members than others. See if it's their personality type which dictates how you work with them, or yours. Personality types are deeply embedded in us (thanks to the influence of Mum, Dad and a few others!). You are unlikely to want or be able to change your essential personality – that's you! – and you must not expect your team members to change theirs.

However, with consideration, you can start to understand why, when you do things differently, they respond differently. Modifying a personality is difficult; modifying a behaviour is also difficult, but it is the easier and more productive of the two!

When you feel that they (and you) are ready for it, get your team members to carry out the same 'What turns you on?' exercise. Let them describe themselves, then similarly describe you. Then compare notes. Do it on a one-to-one basis. As well as creating a bridge between the two of you, you will begin to realise how different your perceptions are of each other and where you chafe. Laugh and have fun. Discuss together how you can both modify your behaviour towards each other, then you can improve how you work together. Your relationships with your team will be powerfully strengthened as a result. You will start to understand them as human beings. The more you understand them, the more effectively you can motivate them.

## Become a master of motivation

Don't be surprised if it takes time and effort to become a master of motivation. But remember, you cannot motivate others if you are not motivated yourself. Motivation has three dimensions – self, team members and team – just as personal relationships have me, you and us. And just as all three dimensions of the personal relationship need time, attention and work, so do the three dimensions of motivation.

## *The Great Brain Robbery*

I have two friends in the USA called Murray Raphel and Ray Considine. Our paths cross from time to time on the international speaking circuits. Murray and Ray used to do occasional double acts and were the life and soul of many a large sales convention. About a decade ago they wrote a book together called *The Great Brain Robbery*. It's an original book suggesting that if we all sit around trying to have good new ideas, the world will run at about half the pace. The book jacket asks, 'How many times have you watched a winner execute a flawless business or sales coup and asked yourself – "How did he do that?"?' *The Great Brain Robbery* then goes on to describe some brilliant business ideas, all of which the authors 'stole' from someone else and invite the reader to steal from them! Well thanks, Murray and Ray, we're about to steal some of your work. It's the bit about WINNERS!

## Motivation makes winners!

Motivation and winning go hand in hand. Winners are motivated. But motivation alone does not make you a winner. Consider this material from *The Great Brain Robbery*.

## W – I – N – N – E – R – S

### W stands for Work

Murray and Ray noticed that winners work smarter than losers. They tell the story of one insurance business that determined to find out why one of their salespeople was writing three times more business than the rest. Apparently they assigned a team of business analysts to follow him around, to listen, to observe and then report back to senior management. And what did they discover about him that made him different to the others? Nothing! He didn't do anything differently. Except, as he said, 'I start fifteen minutes early, I take shorter coffee breaks, I take fifteen minutes less for lunch and I go home fifteen minutes after the others. That way I create an extra hour each day. Five hours a week. Nearly three working days every month. That's a thirteen month year!'

Which leads us to...

### I stands for Ideas

As their book points out, we need to realise that there really is no such thing as a new idea. Actually today's new ideas are really a blend of old ideas reformulated to create a new manifestation, a new concept, a new way. Winners tend to have a constant stream of ideas: ideas about new things to do or try; new things to improve methods or processes; new ways to communicate or work. Working in an environment that welcomes and worships your ideas is incredibly motivating.

**Become an ideas person!**

Idea generation takes place from five simple steps.

1. People who have lots of ideas – ideas people – tend to be those who fill their minds with relevant or interesting information. They read a lot, they talk (that is, they listen!) to people and they watch the world.
2. Ideas people play with all the information in their heads. They experiment, connecting the previously unconnected; or turn facts and information on its head to see how it looks or fits in some other form.
3. Ideas people believe in what I call 'cooking time'. That's the time we give our brain to 'cook' things. The subconscious part of our brains is far bigger than the conscious part, and much more powerful. When you leave ideas to 'cook', you give the larger part of your brain time to work on concepts, thoughts and notions.
4. This is the Eureka moment. It often happens at the most unsuspecting or unlikely times: on the loo, or in the bath! For almost 20 years I used to get stuck at a particularly busy level crossing. I could be stuck there for ten minutes with regular monotony. I eventually began to value that time; it was as if my brain became trained (excuse the pun!) to dream up an idea when those barriers were down.
5. This is the testing time, when we take our new ideas out for a spin. We bounce them off others, and put them into motion to see if they work. Winners stay very flexible at this stage. An idea, in itself, is not something to be cherished and preserved; it is simply the next step to the next idea!

## N stands for Now

Everest was first climbed by Edmund Hillary and Sherpa Tenzing. Who were in the next party to climb it? Who was the second person to land on the moon? After some thought you might recall from your memory banks that is was Buzz Aldrin. But who was second to fly across the Atlantic?

So what's the point? The point is that winning is about being first. Winners attach no merit to being second and don't understand the meaning of the word procrastination. They make decisions and they get things done. The challenge placed before readers of *The Great Brain Robbery* is an interesting one. They suggest you try seeing what happens to your life when you give an answer to every question you are asked – right then and there.

People who have gone along with this concept report that it unclogs their lives. And that their decision making, while it seems scarily impulsive at first, improves because greater emphasis is given to the wisdom of the subconscious brain. That's why you often observe that winners seem to know exactly what they want from life. Perhaps they know their inner selves, which is a valuable requirement for self motivators.

### N stands for Natural

This is probably a direct continuation of the last point. Winners do things with grace, style and a confident ease which leave many people standing, watching, jaws agape. A motivated person is a joy to behold. Think of your favourite sports people. Have you ever known a winner who was clumsy or awkward?

### E stands for Energy

Winners seem to have boundless energy yet they are human like the rest of us, so where does it come from? Certainly feeling motivated releases added energy in us, but the real truth is that winners understand that energy is a limited commodity. So they use it carefully. First, most winners take care of themselves – they keep themselves fit and eat and drink sensibly. Second, they understand the need to delegate. When you are overloaded the quality of your work falls and it is seriously de-motivating. Be warned! If you delegate to someone else and clog them up, you have simply passed your de-motivation to the other person. And that is not good management.

Unclogging your brain and prioritising your time is motivational. Most people have heard of the ABC method where, in simple terms, you divide all your work into three piles or categories: (A) things that MUST be done today; (B) those that could be done tomorrow; and (C) those that could be done next week. Then you ask yourself the question:

'Why should I be doing something today that doesn't need to be done today?' You then have a clearly prioritised set of tasks for that day.

The more radical of the many versions of this concept actually suggest that you throw away the C pile altogether! And I know people who do this. However, they sensibly caution that with such short term and tactical day-by-day decision making about the focus of your time, you need to keep a steady eye on the strategic path and make sure you stay on it.

Recognise the important connection between energy, enthusiasm and motivation. When we feel good about what we do, enjoying it and being excited about the tasks or day ahead of us, we feel motivated.

$$Motivation = enthusiasm = energy!$$

Equally,

$$Enthusiasm = energy = motivation!$$

## R is for Repeat

Winners have the wisdom to work out what they're doing right – and what they're doing wrong. Once they've modelled out the successful behaviours and ideas, they do them again, and again, as long as the ideas keep on working. Winners don't throw good ideas away; they may improve them, recycle them or update them – but they still continue to use them.

> 66 *After one day without practising, I notice. After two days, the critics notice. After three days, the audience stop coming to see me!* 99
> **– A famous violinist, asked about the importance of practising – and how often he practised.**

## S stands for Success

Winners love success. They are passionate about their achievements. They tell all their friends, acquaintances, and even people they meet in the street! Winners are proud of what they do. And they are proud of the way their teams succeed and develop and grow with them. Motivated managers make this happen in their teams. They excite, and enthuse. They support, they counsel and they coach. And they constantly, constantly MOTIVATE.

> ❝ *One change I made with WINNERS is to make the 'E' stand for Enthusiasm. Because that IS what makes the difference in managing people. There's nothing as contagious as enthusiasm. So I'd recommend that change.* ❞
> **– Murray Raphel, American marketer, author and speaker**

You decide!

The best way to become a winner yourself is to create a team of winners. Let your people make you the success you want to be. It never fails! But to be a winner or build a team of winners you need to harness the incredible power of motivation.

1. Creating motivation is a vital task of management. You cannot motivate others if you are not motivated yourself. Motivation is a feeling. Motivation is catching!
2. Motivation is getting people cheerfully, willingly and professionally to do the things the business requires them to do.
3. Motivation is achieved formally and environmentally. The formal method consists of exercises and procedures. The environmental method is created by the atmosphere at work, which is mostly developed by management style.
4. Motivational management is about helping people to know what to do rather than telling them what to do. It is about developing people and letting your people make you the success you want to be.
5. Motivation = enthusiasm = energy
   and enthusiasm = energy = motivation!
6. Winning is about being first. Winning is highly motivational.

## Coming up in this chapter

*What motivates people?*
*Why incentives or money are rarely the right solution*
*How can motivation improve performance?*

## What motivates people?

Most managers have little idea of where they should start with motivating themselves or their staff. And in the old 'command and control' environment it was perceived as unnecessary. If people didn't achieve they were simply moved on or moved out.

Over the past 30 years or so a great deal of work has been done on trying to understand human motivation. Perhaps the most fundamental but also the most useful work was done by three people. Abraham H. Maslow created his now famous Hierarchy of Human Needs. This was further developed by Douglas McGregor and, later still, some work on factors affecting our attitudes to work was published in the *Harvard Business Review* by Frederick Herzberg. Let's take a simplified look at these three hypotheses and see what they tell us. We'll start, therefore, with Maslow's Hierarchy of Human Needs, which is reproduced as Figure 2.1.

---

### Self-Motivation Exercise 1

How well do you understand what motivates you and your team members? Make a list for each of your team noting their three biggest de-motivators. Reflect on how you can help to ease or eradicate these issues. Better still, have a discussion with each to see if your assumptions are correct, then talk about how you can both work to ease or eradicate them. Then do the same for yourself.

---

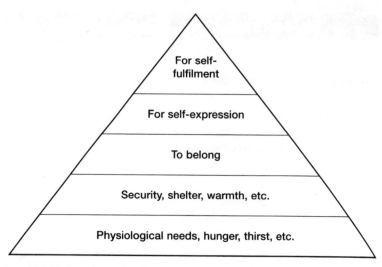

Figure 2.1 Maslow's hierarchy of human needs (*Source:* Abraham H. Maslow, *Motivation and Personality*, Copyright 1954 Harper & Row Inc. Reprinted by permission of HarperCollins Publishers)

Maslow's thesis was fairly simple. As you look at the triangle or pyramid, you will see sets of human needs. The theory is that, working from the bottom up, as each set of needs was met, so the next level of needs established itself. As our bodily needs for food and water were met, we then craved security, shelter and warmth.

Given these, our next need was to belong. If we felt we belonged, then we searched for self-expression and finally – if we could express ourselves – self-fulfilment became the priority. The top three layers of the triangle are where the major emphasis lies for motivation – in the bounds of 'belonging' (this is why teams ultimately will bring out more of an individual's performance), self-expression and self-fulfilment. It is important to appreciate that you can't move up into the top three of Maslow's pyramid unless the bottom two are in place and effective.

## Where does money fit in?

Remuneration falls into the two bottom layers; however, consider why one might descend the hierarchy as well as why one might climb it. It has been my experience that money – in connection with motivation – becomes far more of an issue when the top three layers of the hierarchy (belonging, self-expression and self-fulfilment) are deficient or failing. It is almost as though, when one of our layers is taken away – or that level of needs is not met – we compensate on the layer below. If that isn't strong enough we continue to descend to a level we find comfortable and wallow around in that level, compensating ourselves with extra need gratification.

However, people may drift in and out of needing money. Of course we all need it. But things can happen – divorce, illness, childrens' needs – which change our situation. Does this mean you can't motivate a person who is strapped for cash? Probably. And it means you need to change what you do for them. For example support, understanding, being there and listening will all become increasingly valued. Motivation will not really return until the individual has solved his or her own problem.

---

In the next chapter I will introduce you to my Motivation Maps. I was working with a manager, Chris, once where, in his map, money dominated everything. I knew this wasn't how he felt most of the time. Something was wrong.

I enquired gently about his personal life. It transpired that Chris and his wife had split up over an affair he had embroiled himself in. Now he was living with his lover and trying to keep two homes going. Until he resolved his personal situation, money would remain a problem. To keep him motivated, I had to support him through his problems and counsel him as best I could. A year or so later, Chris had settled in with his new lady who had found herself a job. His divorce was through and a financial settlement agreed which, although it had not made his life easy, had made having one possible. He was getting back on track. As we sat again doing his annual map 'rebuild' it was transformed. The 'old' Chris was on the way back. We both felt good about it, and smiled together as we noticed the difference.

---

Cash-based incentives have been badly discredited and demonstrated to have poor and short-term effects. Let us consider a few experiences on this point, because it will serve to demonstrate why, as motivators, managers should concentrate in the three upper ranges where they will have the greatest success, for there lie such needs as achievement and accomplishment.

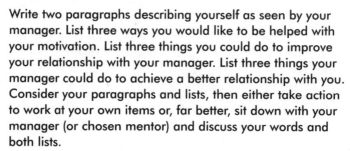

**Self-Motivation Exercise 2**

Write two paragraphs describing yourself as seen by your manager. List three ways you would like to be helped with your motivation. List three things you could do to improve your relationship with your manager. List three things your manager could do to achieve a better relationship with you. Consider your paragraphs and lists, then either take action to work at your own items or, far better, sit down with your manager (or chosen mentor) and discuss your words and both lists.

Before you finish be sure to have exchanged ideas on how what you have learned about each other can improve the way you work together.

## Why incentives are rarely the right solution

Competitions and incentives are often used as part of the motivation process. Everyone might like to win a trip to Hawaii, but who really wins with competitions? Only the competition winners! Incentives like these only really boost performance from those top performing few who think they have a chance – in other words, those who least need incentives in the first place. The result is a short-term boost which, for motivation or team building, usually does nothing that has any prolonged effect on the whole workforce.

❝ *I am a relatively inexperienced salesperson. But I'm learning fast. I found the annual sales competition actually de-motivated me. I knew I had no chance of winning so I didn't even bother. I was more turned on by watching my own improvements. And as for teamwork – forget it. The top guys were all scrabbling to out-do each other!* ❞
**– Martina Peck, sales representative, Southern Cosmetics**

Money as a motivator tends to attract the greedy, the self-centred and the status driven; at the extreme, these are essentially selfish people who would do and say anything to build their earnings. They are, of course, the last people to think about the business, it's Customers or their co-workers.

What do you do if money becomes an issue for someone – if they feel they are being undervalued or underpaid?

Then you must be firm with them and encourage them to make a decision. Their options are clear: ask for more – and if they get it, be content. If they don't, they need to make a radial change seeking somewhere else where they might be satisfactorily rewarded or consider a career change. I have not used the word 'radical' meaning it to sound negative. I have known many people who have chosen radical solutions and moved on to something which they could get passionate about. The return of passion alone brought their motivation roaring back!

The final option is to accept their current situation and to concentrate and build on the positive areas of their life and work.

You must act in these situations – a de-motivated person will be like a rotten apple and their state erodes the motivation of their work-mates.

## How can motivation improve performance?

Let's take our understanding of motivation a little further and see what Douglas McGregor added to Maslow's concept. As we do you will begin to see the benefit of being able to tap into your team members' desires and abilities to self-motivate – and, indeed, your own, for that matter.

The task of the manager is to create the environment and conditions in which self-motivation will flourish and grow. McGregor sought to demonstrate this with his landmark work 'The XY Theory'.

X and Y represent two different extremes of treating people. From Figure 2.2 you will recognise X as the 'old fashioned' way and Y as the 'enlightened' way. X and Y people are not people

Figure 2.2 McGregor's XY theory (from *The Human Side of Enterprise*, McGraw-Hill, 1960)

| The X group | The Y group |
|---|---|
| 1 People dislike work and will avoid it if they can | 1 Work is necessary to people's psychological growth |
| 2 People must be forced or bribed to put out the right effort | 2 People want to be interested in their work and, under the right conditions, they can enjoy it |
| 3 People would rather be directed than accept responsibility, which they avoid | 3 People will direct themselves towards an accepted target |
| | 4 People will seek, and accept, responsibility under the right conditions |
| | 5 The discipline people impose on themselves is more effective, and can be more severe, than any imposed on them |
| 4 People are motivated mainly by money | 6 Under the right conditions people are motivated by the desire to realise their own potential |
| 5 People are motivated by their anxiety about their security | |
| 6 Most people have little creativity – except when getting round management rules | 7 Creativity and ingenuity are widely distributed and grossly under-used |

who like one style or the other or who are naturally positive or negative in their outlook. They are people who have come to feel this way because of the treatment they receive and the environment in which they work.

Those working in an 'X' environment will need to be carefully watched with strict rules, tight discipline and bonuses and incentives regularly applied. X people are highly unmotivated, largely unhappy and often rebellious. They find work a chore, feel their creativity is unwanted and undervalued, feel that they have no voice and that the system is there to make them obey the rules. All of which is, of course, true. In the 1960s, 1970s and even the 1980s, there were many workforces of this type, which is why, money – particularly commission – became so vital to their fabric. I might not be happy – but I'm rich!

In contrast, those people working in a Y environment will be managed by what is known as 'tight/loose controls' (see page 50). They will be encouraged to develop, will feel empowered, be given responsibility and be enabled to succeed. Y people will be high in motivation, self-esteem, confidence and capability.

Y people feel enlightened. They contribute creatively and with initiative. They go that extra mile without anyone needing to ask them to. Y people are enjoying themselves and are stimulated and fulfilled by their work. Their ideas are welcome and they can feel the difference they make. Staff feel trusted, cared for, thought about, valued and appreciated. This is a highly motivational environment in which to work. Work is a pleasure and enhances their lives.

> To be an effective motivational manager you should foster belief system Y. You have a major influence in creating an invigorating environment for your team. Create an environment that breeds and encourages the Y response from your staff and it will bring out the best in them.

## The motivation leverage points

In 1968, the *Harvard Business Review* published a paper by Frederick Herzberg entitled 'One more time: how do you motivate employees?'. Herzberg explains that the key leverage for motivation lies in the satisfaction factors which are most important to us: achievement, recognition, the work itself, responsibility, advancement and growth. This is demonstrated in Figure 2.3, where you can see what turns us on, and by how much.

> Ask what each of these factors mean to your staff. You will get a whole range of different answers. Your own answers will be different too. Once you know the answers to these questions you are in prime position to start understanding their motivation and, together, build their personal motivation maps as described in the following chapter.

Be absolutely clear from Figure 2.3 what the major motivational leverage factors are for both yourself and your team. Knowing these you will: gain a sense of team and personal achievement; give recognition to both the team and individuals

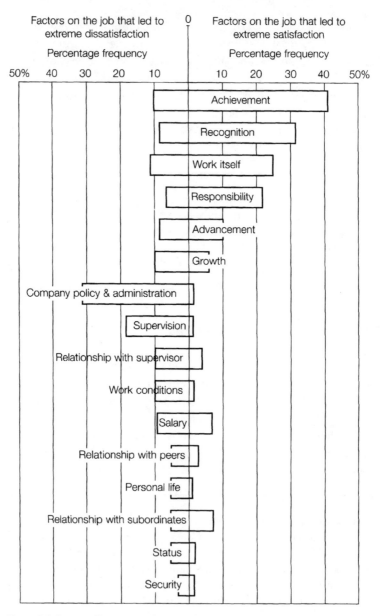

Figure 2.3 Factors affecting attitudes to work (*Source: Fredercik Herzberg, Harvard Business Review 1968*))

within it; make the team and personal work enjoyable (and, yes, that means you can have fun!); devolve responsibility, so you don't keep it all for yourself 'because you are the manager after all'; and assist your team members to advance and develop in their personal and professional lives.

---

### Beware the 'hygiene factors'!

Remember, in order to motivate people using the top three sections of Maslow's pyramid, you have to ensure that the two bottom sets of needs are met. Herzberg referred indirectly to these as the 'hygiene factors'. At work, these basic needs are working conditions, basic pay and benefits, the corporate culture, status, job security and a reasonable personal, social and working life.

You can't use these as motivators because they are *prerequisite* to motivation. Be warned! Get them wrong and they will become 'demotivators'. Get them right and the foundations for motivation are in place. This applies to you as well as the team you manage.

---

Herzberg made the point that the 'hygiene factors' simply remove unhappiness; they don't actually make people happy. Think back and you'll remember just how short the 'buzz' from that salary rise or new car lasted. It's not long. It's no surprise that Herzberg referred to the issues on the top right of his diagram as 'the motivators'.

1. The most effective motivation work will take place in the top three sectors of Maslow's Hierarchy of Human Needs – belonging, self-expression and fulfilment. However, the lowest two levels of basic needs must be successfully in place before this is possible.
2. Incentives and money rarely provide long-term motivation of any substance – salary and commission fall into the two lower Maslow categories. They are among other 'hygiene factors' such as: working conditions, benefits, corporate culture, status, job security, and so on.
3. McGregor's XY theory explains how people can self-motivate and be motivated given the right environment and culture – empowerment, creativity and a sense of purpose and growth.

4. The key leverage for motivation lies in the factors which are most important to us at work: achievement, recognition, the work itself, responsibility, advancement and growth.

## Coming up in this chapter

*The secret of 3D motivation*
*Motivation maps*
*Motivation map introductory exercise*

## The route ahead

Motivation works in three dimensions: self, team member and team. In this chapter we will concentrate on the team member and team elements, as these will be the backbone of your formal motivational work and exercises. However, you can't motivate others if you are not motivated yourself and therefore the last chapter is dedicated entirely to 'self'.

Many of the things we're going to look at next work just as well for you personally as they do for your team. That means you should expect your manager to be working at such activities with and for you. I repeat, if he or she doesn't – shout!

---

I am a great advocate of reading to expand your own personal skills and development. Many books are available. One of the best, written by a friend, American Jinny Ditzler, is called *Your Best Year Yet* (Thorsons 1994). I thoroughly recommend it. Incidentally, I also believe you can learn a lot about motivation from simple observation of people – anytime, anywhere!

---

I have stated that the key to motivating your team members is to know, understand and appreciate them as human beings. Then, as you learn about each member you will be able to construct their motivation maps. But what is a motivation map? Simply put, it is the chart upon which you can plot your course to the perfect motivation mix for all three dimensions. These maps will enable you to see a picture of the nature and mix of motivational work and activity that you need to do for each team member and with your team as a whole. I cannot stress too strongly the power of motivation maps if they are created and used vigorously.

You will also be able to see your own personal needs. You will be able to provide some of the requirements that emerge for yourself. Simply place them into the category of self-motivational activities. You will need to discuss others with your manager to ensure that you receive them.

Construct a map for each team member and one for your team as a whole. From these you will be able to monitor and create motivational work and activity and monitor your own managerial effectiveness.

## Introducing the Motivation Map

I'm going to give you a template to work from. It is NOT the ultimate; you can and should develop it further. Once a map exists for each team member, I have an exercise you can use with them (as a team) to enable you to track down some more motivational factors. To start our mapping process let's return to Herzberg's factors about work that led to extreme satisfaction or dissatisfaction. The list, in the order of magnitude, is given in Figure 3.1 (see page 32).

We'll be working with Hertzberg's top five – achievement, recognition, work itself, responsibility and advancement – plus one other chosen by the individual or team whose map you are preparing. To find a sixth, you should write the list given in Figure 3.1 and show it to each individual. Explain that you have already selected the five you wish to work on and that you would like them to choose as a sixth – something which is important to them at this time. Do not reveal Herzberg's percentage frequencies; let them choose in ignorance of the research. If they suggest something that has not appeared on Herzberg's list, that's fine.

**What happens if they want to add 'money' to the list?**

Remember Chris and his financial problems trying to keep two households? If one of your team should want to add money as part of their motivation, that's fine. As with all the other factors, discuss it with them and find out why. You may not be able to pay them more – or enough to solve the problem – even if you want to, but at least you can be aware of their need and how it is affecting their motivation. And you can offer support of the non-financial kind.

Beware, money can also be used as a smoke screen to hide the real issues because they may be more intimate and personal. For some, these are more difficult to discuss.

In the case of a greedy person, money is the true answer. You will have to consider such a person very carefully because their motivation may never harmonise with the rest of the team – or the culture of the business.

My experience is that 'new' ideas usually fit into one of Herzberg's originals and are not genuinely new factors in themselves. It's of no matter, so discuss their choice with them. Once you have made sure it is a robust choice, enter it as the sixth on their list. Next ask them to place the six items in what they consider to be the order of importance.

**Playing with motivation maps**

It's easy and fun – and you can develop both individual and team exercises to help you and your team understand their own motivation. Be inventive with these – turn them into games for example.

Many people have a subconscious acceptance of what motivates them. Your task, as well as increasing your own awareness of what enthuses them as individuals, is to bring that into their own conscious thinking so that they become more able to self-motivate. This gives the whole process a further boost. Not only will they understand themselves better but they will also recognise that you do too and that you are working to help their performance.

When you have completed this, you are ready to create the basic map. However, against each of the six headings you can now add a list of items from their work which make up the sub-factors contributing to their scores in each main factor category.

**ADVANCEMENT**

| | | | | | |
|---|---|---|---|---|---|
| Job status | [1] | [2] | [3] | [4] | [5] |
| Career plans and objectives | [1] | [2] | [3] | [4] | [5] |
| Promotion | [1] | [2] | [3] | [4] | [5] |
| Training and self-improvement | [1] | [2] | [3] | [4] | [5] |
| Helping train new people | [1] | [2] | [3] | [4] | [5] |
| Temporary team leadership (during holidays, and sickness) | [1] | [2] | [3] | [4] | [5] |
| Job experience or secondment | [1] | [2] | [3] | [4] | [5] |
| Help with skills or qualifications | [1] | [2] | [3] | [4] | [5] |

**RESPONSIBILITY**

| | | | | | |
|---|---|---|---|---|---|
| More job responsibility | [1] | [2] | [3] | [4] | [5] |
| More involvement with corporate issues | [1] | [2] | [3] | [4] | [5] |
| Team or departmental development work | [1] | [2] | [3] | [4] | [5] |
| Less supervision | [1] | [2] | [3] | [4] | [5] |
| Involvement in planning | [1] | [2] | [3] | [4] | [5] |
| Involvement in team training/coaching | [1] | [2] | [3] | [4] | [5] |
| Involvement with special activities or projects | [1] | [2] | [3] | [4] | [5] |
| Stand-in leader at meetings | [1] | [2] | [3] | [4] | [5] |

**WORK ITSELF**

| | | | | | |
|---|---|---|---|---|---|
| Involvement in team decisions | [1] | [2] | [3] | [4] | [5] |
| On the job support | [1] | [2] | [3] | [4] | [5] |
| Team spirit | [1] | [2] | [3] | [4] | [5] |
| Less routine and boredom (or more variety) | [1] | [2] | [3] | [4] | [5] |
| Freedom to work my own way | [1] | [2] | [3] | [4] | [5] |
| Job clarity/definition | [1] | [2] | [3] | [4] | [5] |
| Pride | [1] | [2] | [3] | [4] | [5] |

Figure 3.1 JFR's motivation maps, a template

For the factor they chose themselves you should debate with them five or six sub-factors which contribute to their motivation, so that this topic matches the others on the template.

Remember, the 'I' from WINNERS was to have IDEAS. Don't be lazy with the motivation maps. I have never met a successful manager who was lazy. Don't accept this template just as it stands. Create your own geared to the work of your team. For example, under 'achievement' you could include 'volume targets' or perhaps 'Customer satisfaction', 'meeting deadlines', and so on.

| | | | | | |
|---|---|---|---|---|---|
| Enthusiasm | [1] | [2] | [3] | [4] | [5] |
| Measurable standards of performance | [1] | [2] | [3] | [4] | [5] |

**RECOGNITION**

| | | | | | |
|---|---|---|---|---|---|
| Regular feedback | [1] | [2] | [3] | [4] | [5] |
| Regular communication | [1] | [2] | [3] | [4] | [5] |
| More praise | [1] | [2] | [3] | [4] | [5] |
| Less criticism | [1] | [2] | [3] | [4] | [5] |
| Incentives, prizes and rewards | [1] | [2] | [3] | [4] | [5] |
| Status and job titles, etc. | [1] | [2] | [3] | [4] | [5] |
| Salary increases and bonuses | [1] | [2] | [3] | [4] | [5] |
| League tables | [1] | [2] | [3] | [4] | [5] |
| Recognition tokens (dinners, events,etc.) | [1] | [2] | [3] | [4] | [5] |
| Access, time and availability of manager | [1] | [2] | [3] | [4] | [5] |

**ACHIEVEMENT**

| | | | | | |
|---|---|---|---|---|---|
| Self-created targets and plans | [1] | [2] | [3] | [4] | [5] |
| Hitting targets/goals | [1] | [2] | [3] | [4] | [5] |
| Contribution to profitability/ productivity | [1] | [2] | [3] | [4] | [5] |
| Project work | [1] | [2] | [3] | [4] | [5] |
| Achievement feedback, reports and talks | [1] | [2] | [3] | [4] | [5] |

**SELF-CHOSEN CATEGORY**

| | | | | | |
|---|---|---|---|---|---|
| Sub-factor 1 | [1] | [2] | [3] | [4] | [5] |
| Sub-factor 2 | [1] | [2] | [3] | [4] | [5] |
| Sub-factor 3 | [1] | [2] | [3] | [4] | [5] |
| Sub-factor 4 | [1] | [2] | [3] | [4] | [5] |
| Sub-factor 5 | [1] | [2] | [3] | [4] | [5] |
| Sub-factor 6 | [1] | [2] | [3] | [4] | [5] |

This template is not one created especially for you or your team. Challenge it. Discuss it with your team. You may find other sub-factors to include beneath Herzberg's motivational factors. Mould it! Shape it! Make it yours! Own it with your team. It's a great tool because there are no right or wrong answers.

> **Explore and debate your team members' selections. For example, let's suppose one of the team has identified 'career' as their sixth factor. Find out why. Discuss it. Ask questions like 'Why is career so important to you?', 'What aspects of your career concern you?', 'Why do you feel like that?' and 'How does that connect to your motivation level?'.**

**A thought you might find useful**

Try to use this discretely and occasionally. Sometimes in these kinds of discussions people get a little coy and hide their feelings with sheepish grins saying, 'I don't know'. Promptly slide this in – 'Well, if you did know the answer, what would it be?' Sometimes they look at you as if you're nuts and respond with 'What a stupid question!' but more usually the right answer just pops out!

Next, ask them to score each individual sub-factor on the sheet out of five, representing the importance of that sub-factor as it relates to their own understanding of what motivates them. The lower the score, the lower they rate it for their own motivation. You then have a comprehensive view of their primary motivation factors, why they are important, what can and should be done about them, and where they can be improved upon. You can also consider what behaviour changes need to take place or be modified to boost motivation. Give them a copy of the sheet and retain one yourself. This will become the map of your motivational plans for them. The individual plans may then be combined to create a team understanding.

**Get mapping!**

My advice is that, once created, your team members' individual maps and the map for the team as a whole should be systematically worked on, reviewed and updated at least once a year. You may use it in their formal appraisal. However, it is preferable to discuss one of the top motivators with your team members at least once a quarter.

Start taking an interest, if you don't already, in the psychological issues of your role as a manager. A friend who has taught and trained in many guises over the years, came to a firm conclusion that coaching, mentoring, groupwork and interactive learning processes (role-play, for example) were by far the most effective. I challenged her about this one day. First she spouted figures at me about the 'absorption rate' and 'retention rate' of information, then she laughed and said, 'Anyway, I know it's the most effective way because every fanatical cult and sect in the world uses it'.

## A motivation map exercise

This exercise is based on one that I have used for many years in my counselling work. It adapts well to many circumstances and, if you approach it sensitively and thoughtfully, will work well for you as a part of your teamwork. You can use it alone or in conjunction with the motivation maps and it should provide you with valuable insights into the motivational support your team will need from you. And why not include yourself in the exercise? That will tell your team that they can immediately help to motivate you.

### Team level

In a relaxed atmosphere sit for some groupwork with your team, preferably in a circle (such as round a table – but avoid becoming the 'head' of it). Ask them to cut or tear an A4 sheet into four (A6) pieces. Then, from the five main Herzberg factors (achievement, recognition, and so on), together with the sixth factor they have chosen, ask them to write one factor secretly on each of the four pieces – in effect their personal selection of their four most important factors. Then they should place them face down on the table.

To do this they have obviously discarded the two they consider least important. If they have difficulty, be patient and discuss any dilemmas. Next ask them to discard another two of their selection and place the remaining two face down on the table. They will then have selected their two most important personal motivational factors. Go round the group, asking each member to turn the least important of his or her two final selections face up. One by one, get them to discuss why this is important and how they would like you to work on it with them as part of the team. Then go round again in exactly the same way, asking them to discuss their final and therefore most important personal factor. Again encourage discussion and thought about their needs.

Encourage your team to continue discussing their similarities and differences. Ask them if you can write down their two top choices. If they agree, do so. If they object, use your memory and note them privately later. Hold on to these choices and ensure that your future motivational teamwork addresses the needs you have uncovered. Later, check to see how their choices match their motivation maps. If they are different, discuss whether this is a change and find out which is the current order of priority. If the order has changed, create an updated version.

When working on motivation, make sure that everyone is listening intently. Discourage individuals from interrupting or talking over each other, and create what counsellors often refer to as a 'safe' environment. This means simply that there should be a feeling of safety to discuss personal thoughts, attitudes and feelings.

### Sub-factor level

I suggest this work is best done on an individual basis. As it gets more detailed, it also gets more intimate. The idea is to repeat the exercise above, perhaps taking one main factor a month. This time they should select four of the sub-factors from the chosen motivation factor of the month. Keep this up. As you meet their needs, other issues emerge and take higher or lower priorities. Once a year, audit them with a blank map and ask them to do it again. Discuss any changes. And, where there hasn't been change, ask them (and yourself) why. This means that your motivation work has not made any noticeable difference.

### Don't just leave it there

As a result of motivation map exercises and games there will be learning and awareness, but you have to make sure that the result is action. Develop an action plan for the team and for the individuals. Create measurable objectives. Give them dates for review and completion. That way you will see these things as actionable activities and record your successes. Make progress visible and tangible.

1. Motivation maps need to be prepared in all three dimensions: yourself, each individual team member and a composite for the team.
2. A motivation map charts a person's feelings about their most important personal priorities; what motivates them.
3. Motivation maps should be consulted regularly, used to develop teams and team members and be updated at least annually.
4. The maps can also be used to diagnose the motivation issues that don't change and, therefore, highlight the further discussion and planning that is necessary.
5. Motivation maps can be used in team work, but at the sub-factor level it should be one to one – manager and team member.
6. Don't forget about action plans and measurable objectives. Make progress visible and tangible.

## Coming up in this chapter

*Changing behaviour*
*Creating rapport*
*Making the most of appraisals*
*Giving feedback*
*Leading the way*

In order to understand motivation and to build our skill in creating and sustaining it there are a number of areas we need to consider. These skills include changing behaviour, building rapport with and within the team, handling appraisals, giving feedback and perfecting your leadership style. Mishandling any of these will seriously hinder or erode motivation. Get them right and both you and your team will benefit, feel good and, as a result, be better motivated.

## Changing behaviour, improving performance

People are sometimes curious beings. For example, think about our decision making in relation to our behaviour – why we do things and why we don't. If behaviour was about logic, no one would smoke and everyone would wear their seatbelts and abide by the speed limits. Dr Aubrey C. Daniels, a US specialist and the author of *Bringing out the Best in People* (McGraw-Hill 1994), describes the 'ABC theory of behavioural change'.

Behavioural change is broken down into three steps:

○ **A**ntecedent – *something that occurs prior to and provokes a behaviour*
○ **B**ehaviour – *what a person does*
○ **C**onsequence – *what happens to that person as a result of their behaviour*

Consequences are viewed from three perspectives:

○ *Positive or negative – in the view of the person's whose behaviour you seek to modify*

❍ *Immediate or future – does the consequence happen immediately as the behaviour changes or at some time in the future?*

❍ *Certain or uncertain – is it guaranteed that the consequence will occur or is it doubtful or uncertain?*

A change in behaviour is most likely to occur when the outcome or consequence is positive, immediate and certain. Where the consequence is negative, in the future or uncertain, behavioural change is unlikely. 'I <u>might</u> <u>die</u> of smoking <u>when</u> <u>I'm</u> <u>older</u>', for example, or, 'If I drive without my seatbelt fastened, <u>one day</u> I <u>might</u> be <u>injured</u>.' The less positive, less certain and further into the future the consequence, the less likely behaviour is to change.

> Poor performance requires people to modify their behaviour to create an improved or different outcome. Poor performance is usually caused by a skill problem – they are unable to do it – or a motivational problem – they are unwilling do it. To cure a skill problem you can coach, train or develop. To cure a motivational problem, you have to understand it and solve it by creating a positive consequence for the required change in behaviour.

Dr Daniels explains that the only person who can change an individual's behaviour is the individual themselves. This is a vital realisation if you wish people to adopt different behaviour to improve their performance. We have to appreciate that managing the consequences of behaviour is the best way to change it.

## Building rapport

Relationships are vastly improved and more effective when good rapport is created. Good rapport simply means that bodies and words match or echo each other. It makes the difference between verbal contact and truly effective communication. Only a small percentage of effective communication is to do with the words used. Effective communication has 7 per cent verbal content and 93 per cent non-verbal.

*❝ Rapport enables people to be at ease or to put others at ease in a range of situations whether in the home or office. It is in the widest sense of the word a social skill. It is also, for a few, a natural and undeveloped skill. For others, it is an unknown or unrecognised facility which can be worked on once awareness has been created and the methods demonstrated. ❞*

**– Russell Webster, consultant and NLP practitioner**

Non-verbal communication breaks down into 38 per cent tone of voice and 55 per cent body influence such as body language, appearance, posture, gesture and eye contact. We all learn verbal skills at school but have no formal education of non-verbal communication. It is left to observation and trial and error. If we get it right people like us: if we don't, they don't! Non-verbal skills, like verbal skills, can be learned, crafted and tuned.

Some people are naturally talented at building rapport. Whether you are or not, you will benefit from increased learning. This includes the use of voice (tone, rhythm and speed), eye movements and body matching. Once accomplished, you will be able to observe the unspoken feelings and desires of your staff with increasing accuracy. You will understand their non-verbal signals and, for example, know when they express agreement but their heart is not behind the words.

Put rapport skills high on your personal development list.

---

**The benefits of talking and sharing in groups build gradually. Trust and safety take time to construct. Openness is not a natural ability for all – especially at work. And it's not always so easy to see failures or failings as opportunities, particularly if you think your manager is going to bite your head off. However, when your team see such discussions leading through to personal and team development and progress which genuinely demonstrates that you are listening to them, thinking about them and anxious to help them, they have tangible proof that they can trust and be open with the group and with you personally. You have helped them positively to solve the problem and have not reacted with a mocking indictment of their inability.**

### Giving effective appraisals

Giving effective formal or informal appraisals is extremely important in the motivation of your team. Many companies operate an annual formal appraisal system and everyone falls in with it. Appraisals are extremely powerful and should be used for discussing personal and business objectives, improving performance, and identifying and planning training and development. They should also include discussions about the individual's future career aspirations and how these fit with the organisation. Importantly, appraisals must be motivational.

---

**The Four 'F's of Appraisals: Fair, Feedback, Fulsome and Frequent**

Do everything in your power to make your appraisals fair. And remember, fair means it must feel fair not just to you but, more importantly, to the person being appraised. If you develop even a suspicion that the recipient feels that anything is unfair, ask them directly and clear it up before you move on.

Feedback should flow in both directions. As well as giving feedback, enquire about your own management style. Above all else, feedback sessions must be open, honest, constructive and safe.

Fulsome refers to praise and to scope. Make sure you use plenty of praise where it's due. Praise – as long as it is sincere and deserved – makes us all feel good. Feeling good is vital for motivation. Fulsome also refers to the scope of your appraisal. Be wide-ranging and include the total performance of the individual. Ensure you cover aspects relating to their contribution to the team and to team spirit as well as their work, quality and attitudes.

Frequent means exactly that – if your business has annual formal appraisals that is fine as a minimum. But used more frequently informal appraisals will benefit both performance and motivation enormously. Appraisals should celebrate success and give people a clear view of what they need to do next.

---

An effective manager will carry out informal appraisals regularly, at least quarterly or more frequently if there are problems or difficulties. These should be carried out with individual team members but you can also use a team appraisal as a team exercise.

Avoid lumping all your appraisals together. Spread them evenly and you'll find that they are of a much better quality.

---

In your appraisals:

❑ Concentrate on the difference you can make to the future, don't get bogged down with the past.
❑ Understand that appraisals are about analysis and development of your team members' skills and competences.
❑ Praise generously as well as discussing the improvements you want.
❑ Together produce measurable objectives with review dates.
❑ Together ensure you end up with a personal development plan.
❑ Specify the next appraisal date – and stick to it!

---

## Giving and receiving feedback

Feedback is a turn-on provided it is given well. It should always lead to a positive and constructive outcome for the recipient, so even negative feedback will be welcome and not worrying.

Giving praise and positive feedback is important. If opportunities don't naturally occur, create them. Managers often forget or overlook things that have gone right and somehow always remember things that have gone wrong.

It is easy and enjoyable for both parties to give positive feedback as long as you don't skate over the good stuff. Savour and discuss it thoroughly so the team member feels fully appreciated. This will reap the full motivation potential and reinforces the behaviour.

Inevitably, an element of your feedback will be critical or negative but even negative feedback can, and should, be given in a helpful and positive way. To assist you in giving negative feedback, use JFR's Nine Golden Rules of Feedback and you will find your communications are cleaner and better received.

1. Always give feedback as quickly as possible after an event.
2. Do not criticise the person. Use your comments to develop an improvement, not to be judgmental. Criticise the process. For example, 'Only an idiot would do it like that!' should be 'Do you think there might be a better way to do that?'.

> **"** *Write people's accomplishments in stone and their faults in sand.* **"**
> **– Benjamin Franklin**

3. Always remind team members before feedback that the aim is positive – you are doing your best to help their development and growth.
4. Make all feedback accurate, factual, specific and constructive.
5. Give feedback openly by stating your feelings and taking responsibility for them. Then ask the team members' views. Listen. Be prepared to debate.
6. Never let tempers become involved. If they should, resolve the issue to restore calm before continuing.
7. Regularly ask for feedback for yourself. It's known as 'upward appraisal'. For example, 'How do you feel about the way I manage?' or 'How do you feel the appraisal went' and 'Have you any suggestions to help me improve that?'
8. Do everything in your power to give negative feedback in a way that leaves the team member feeling valued and appreciated.
9. Always, ALWAYS, **ALWAYS**, **ALWAYS** begin and end in a positive manner.

Positive feedback is a life enhancer. If you can get your life enhanced at work it is deeply motivational. I repeat, if opportunities don't arise to give enough positive feedback, create them.

## Leading the way

The objective of a management team leader is to reach a point where, in terms of the day-to-day work of the team, you are unnecessary – yet absolutely vital. By this I mean that, for the process and content of their work, your team should function without you. The business will continue to flourish. However, you are there for their motivation, energy, enthusiasm and spirit. And for guidance, support and inspiration.

One day I had been working with a longstanding Client and some of his team. As I was about to leave the Client's office, I was aware that he was buzzing with excitement although, to me, it didn't feel as if I had contributed much all day. Intrigued, I mentioned it. The Client felt I had contributed a great deal and it had been, for him, a valuable day. Later, I discussed this day with a friend. 'So why was the Client so happy with my facilitation of the day . . . and, apparently, with me?' I asked. The friend smiled knowingly and left the room, only to return with something from her extensive and wide-ranging library.

My friend was interested in, and fascinated by, people and quality. It didn't matter to her whether books were traditional and conventional or new age, alternative or downright freaky! The book she was clutching came from somewhere between the middle and the downright freaky end of the shelves. It was called the The Tao of Leadership.

The author of The Tao of Leadership is an American named John Heider, a teacher of those who lead groups, boards, teams, and so on. His book is an adaptation of the work of a Chinese philosopher who wrote a work addressed to the 'sage and wise political ruler of China' in the fifth century BC. I knew this was going to be difficult!

**How to become a great leader**
My friend browsed the early pages of the book and handed me a page. 'Let's discuss this', she said. I took the book and looked where her finger pointed on the page. It said this:

> ❝ Of a great leader, the people will say, 'we did it ourselves' ❞
> **– Lao Tzu**

As a manager, you are, first and foremost, a leader. Your greatest resource is your team. You must value and nurture them. If you lead them well, they will lead you to your achievement and your success.

❝ *The fundamental learning point for the leaders in my team is to understand that their true aim is to enable their team members to 'do it themselves'. It is only when our people can do it themselves that they can get in front of Customers being and feeling really confident, supremely competent and knowledgeable – true top of the industry professionals – that we will be doing the best possible job. It's the kind of leader I'm striving to be. It's a really hard thing to learn. To know when to intervene and never to interfere: to appreciate that, as a leader, our task is to serve, nurture and cultivate those who are doing the real work of the business.* ❞

**– Derek Hall, Sales Director, L&M**
**with over 180 sales managers and 1,500 salespeople**

Leadership is about helping others to realise their own potential – empowerment. Add to that the strength, power and commitment that being part of a well led team brings and you will have understood a critical part of your role as a motivator and truly effective manager.

People get a buzz out of being respected, praised, trusted and admired. Through leading and coaching, team members feel the difference: they feel encouraged rather than criticised; they feel supported rather than denigrated; they feel they are being cultivated rather than victimised. They feel MOTIVATED!

I remember the elderly managing director of the very first business I joined as a lowly junior. He believed in 'opening and closing the shop'. The shop was actually an office with three hundred and fifty staff!

'Opening the shop' meant being by the front door from 8.30 a.m. to say good morning to everyone and greet them with a smile. 'Closing the shop' took place from about 4.30 p.m. – it was a walk around the business asking people how their day had gone, saying thank you for the day's work and 'I look forward to seeing you tomorrow'. It was truly appreciated by all and a wonderful contribution to our motivation, loyalty and commitment. He demonstrably cared.

So, what is the meaning of all this to your work? Quite simply, less is more. In other words, your task is not to dictate or order the team to do things. It is about enabling them to do things.

## Help them to know

Successful managers appreciate that clarity of task has a great influence on motivation. If I know what to do and I know how to do it well, my motivation stays high. If I am unclear or have doubts about my task or capability, my motivation will fall.

A key part of being clear about what you have to do is having a clear written job specification which is understood, a clear set of procedures which are rehearsed and embedded and a clear set of job standards which are monitored and where performance can be appreciated. With such monitoring, fairly and professionally carried out and recorded, people's progress can be charted and their continuing development planned and implemented.

Help your team members to see these processes for the valuable self-development opportunities they present. This all forms part of their empowerment process. You are helping them to do their job better, just as your manager must do the same for you, empowering you to take more responsibility with your team and to create a truly motivating atmosphere in which your people enjoy their work.

1. You cannot change someone's behaviour – only they can change it.
2. The three-step behaviour process – antecedent, behaviour, consequence – is most effective when a positive outcome is certain and immediate. The less positive, less certain and further into the future the consequence, the less likely behaviour is to change.
3. Only 7 per cent of communication is verbal. Rapport – the matching of non-verbal communication to the words being spoken – can be crafted and tuned to improve relationships and build communications skills.
4. Appraisals can be given formally – say, annually – and informally, more regularly such as quarterly or even more frequently still. The 'Four F's of Appraisals' are fair, feedback, fulsome and frequent.
5. Giving and receiving feedback should be tackled as quickly as possible after the event; relate feedback to the process or behaviour, not the person; give negative

feedback in a way that the team member still feels valued and appreciated; begin and end positively.

6. As a manager, you are, first and foremost, a leader. Your greatest resource is your team. Leadership is about helping others to realise their fullest potential.

7. Clarity of task is important to motivation. If I know what to do and I know how to do it well, my motivation stays high. If I am unclear or have doubts about my task or capability, my motivation will fall.

## Coming up in this chapter

*Coping with change*
*Worship is within your grasp!*
*Seven tips for the effective manager*
*Five steps to success*

## What we must do next

This chapter is about your management style – its aim is to ensure that you know what best to do to create a motivational environment for your team. Since we live in a business world of constant change, what better place to start?

## Coping with the change

Change is constantly with us these days. Technology, competition, skill shortages, market fluctuations and exchange rates – all manner of turbulence constantly attacks organisations and challenges them to find, new, better, cheaper, faster ways of doing things. As a result businesses are constantly striving to change things for the better.

The trouble with change is that we all have to stop doing what we know how to do and start doing something we don't know how to do, at least not yet. This is why the favourite human reaction to change is that we relate the problems of the present to the solutions of the past. Now, suddenly, they no longer fit.

It can be quite difficult to stop a habit or routine. We experience what works and make it a routine. And, the older we get, or perhaps the longer we go on getting results with something, the more 'right' it feels to us. It's understandable. Keeping motivation high is important during change. You must keep your team's and your own motivation in tip top shape while you change the way you do things.

It will help if you build consensus about the need to change and commitment to the desired outcome. For change to be effective, it is better if it is wanted, rather than just thrust upon us. Think about this in relation to the range of different types of people and experiences that make up a typical team: a whole spectrum of people; a whole rainbow of opinion and ideas; a mass of different experiences and talents. This is exactly the treasure chest within their people that managers should be trying to unlock: a huge resource of experience, skills and pent-up initiative.

When people feel that they are contributing effectively to the desired outcome, they will feel motivated. Also, make the measures of success tangible and visible. There is nothing more motivational than to see yourself making progress, hitting targets and deadlines and getting towards your goals. If your team are not doing as well as you hoped, gather them round you and congratulate them on where they have got. Then work out together how to get back on track. Motivation in this instance will not come from haranguing them about the fact that things are running behind or have gone off track. Constantly stay positive. Build their confidence and energy. Show them how to do better. Encourage and enable. Now you're motoring!

*It was great because we could see just how well we were doing – we had charts and graphs on the walls, a daily update e-mail, faxes from the MD – all sorts of things that kept us informed, kept cheering us on. Well, it sort of super-charged us.*
**– 'Mo' Mobawe, project co-ordinator, Simpson Fuels plc**

### Tight/loose controls

Given the opportunity, freedom and encouragement, people will perform better than they will if they have to adhere to a tight corset of rules, instructions and discipline. This is known as 'tight/loose controls'. It means your goals and targets are clear and precise – tight; but how you achieve them is up to you – loose. People like to be managed in this way and this power is what you are being asked to foster, develop and set free within your team – the power to achieve and excel, and to feel they did it themselves. It is THEIR power.

To succeed, all concerned must commit to it unreservedly. If they have doubts and fears, discuss it with them. Don't ever bury or dismiss doubt. It will hold them and you back. Motivation will sag. Work will suffer. When you believe in it, trust it and commit yourself to it, it will happen.

---

**WORSHIP is within your grasp!**

Effective motivational managers consistently exhibit the following qualities:

**W**orking for you is a pleasure: people love it.
**O**perationally you are admired. You know your job and do it well.
**R**eliability is something you engender. People never feel they could let you down.
**S**ure is how people feel with you. They know where they stand.
**H**elp is always on hand from you. And people know what is expected of them.
**I**mpartial is your middle name. Fairness and equality is spread throughout your team.
**P**anic? Never. You are calm and handle problems thoughtfully.

---

### The Dynamic Dozen – the motivational manager's checklist

**1. Understand how much of your success is governed by your team's motivation**

Creating an exhilarating and enthusiastic atmosphere in which to work and giving people the responsibility to develop and do new and different things, are not always easy, but they are always necessary. Be there when they slip up. Help them to dust themselves off and have another go. Be there when they succeed. Be generous in your praise.

**2. Constantly review your time management**

Put real energy into organising yourself to have as much time as possible with your team, and plenty of that working on motivation.

### 3.  Become a master of feedback

Giving and receiving safe, sincere and deep feedback is a craft. Learn it. Work at it. You will develop a closeness and intimacy, with your team which is at the same time both wonderful and powerful.

### 4.  Develop your people at every possible opportunity

Make people aware of their successes to build their motivation. Build cohesion between your team members' personal aspirations and those of the business. Support and lead them to achieve those aspirations by creating a team atmosphere of personal growth and development. Let learning be celebrated!

### 5.  Concentrate on managing

When you have an office-based team to manage, it takes real concentration on your part not to get sucked into to the day-to-day work. If you manage a field-based team, or if you have a team of home-based people or tele-workers, the task of motivation is going to have to occupy the vast majority of your time. The most motivational times are when you are with them one on one.

> Keeping people motivated is an important component of keeping people. The better you help them to be, the better targets they are for others. If you lose them, all that effort, development work and training is lost to you and lost to the business. Recruiting and training good people is vastly more expensive than managing them well and building their commitment and loyalty to you and to the business.

### 6.  Don't do their job for them, help them to do it themselves

Build motivation and competence within your team. Doing their work for them clogs you up and hinders your ability to give support and guidance and manage effectively. It sends out completely the wrong signals. Your staff need to know you will be there to help and coach them in getting it right. When you take the work from them to do yourself it tells them they are not good enough, that you think they are hopeless and you don't trust them. It's undermines them and is totally, totally de-motivating.

**7.   Understand that you succeed by making others successful**
Use your skills to create people in your mould. Undertake plenty of motivation exercises and activities. Learn to understand what makes them tick and build the best possible relationships with them. Now you are a trainer, a coach, a counsellor, a guide and mentor, and a friend. Support like this is sensationally motivational. Their success will be yours.

---

I will never forget my first meeting with someone who has since become a much valued friend. It was about fifteen years ago when I was a director of a group of companies. He was an extremely talented management consultant who I had invited into the business to give us the benefit of his advice. By way of introduction I took him on a tour of the buildings showing him all various pieces of machinery and equipment we had. As we returned to my office I sat down at my desk and proudly told him, "There is nothing any- where in these buildings I can't run. From printing presses to computers to the switchboard to the fork lifts. I never ask anyone to do anything I can't do myself. I might not do it as well as they can. But at least I can do it."

The management consultant fixed me with a look. "You idiot", he said.

---

**8.   Work hard at understanding the cultural change that is taking place**
It is happening not just in your business, but in all businesses. Transform your management style to adapt to the business culture. Remember that people react to the way they are treated. The most effective atmosphere is in the manner of the McGregor 'Y' culture (page 24).

**9.   Don't underestimate the power of clarity of purpose on motivation**
Remember these words:

*If I know what to do and I know how to do it well, my motivation stays high. If I am unclear or have doubts about my task or capability, my motivation will fall.*

**10. Before you decide anything, ask yourself: Is this good or bad for motivation?**
When a negative answer rears its ugly head, find the positive motivational way to approach and overcome it. That is really managing!

**11. Take yourself seriously – you are a work of art**
Know yourself. Look at the skills that make you a brilliant manager. Use them to develop and improve your team. Look at your weaknesses. Welcome the identification of these for what it is – a learning opportunity. Then vigorously set about changing things.

> ❝ *The human resource is increasingly being recognised as a key source of competitive leverage.* ❞
> **– Institute of Personal Development**

**12. Understand that the very qualities which made you excel at what you did before becoming a manager are probably precisely the qualities of successful management**
Think about this one. It's important. Businesses do not promote people to manage unless they are good. Such qualities will likely include the ability to:

- ○ *listen*
- ○ *create rapport*
- ○ *relate to people*
- ○ *communicate*
- ○ *focus on high leverage points*
- ○ *absorb new ideas and concepts*
- ○ *understand and encourage change*
- ○ *make things happen*
- ○ *accept and master new methods, techniques and skills*
- ○ *coach, mentor and be a good leader*

If you feel you have any weaknesses in that list, make it a priority to develop yourself as you feel necessary. If in doubt take feedback and guidance from those who appointed you – and, if you feel comfortable about it, from your team too.

1. Keeping motivation high is important during change. For change to be effective, it is better if it is wanted, rather than just thrust upon us.
2. Given the opportunity, freedom and encouragement, people will perform better than they will if given a tight corset of rules, instructions and discipline. It's known as 'tight/loose controls'
3. People will WORSHIP you if you: make work a pleasure; know your job and do it well; never let people down; let people know where they stand; help people out; be impartial, fair and equal; and never panic.
4. The Dynamic Dozen – the motivational manager's checklist:
    1. Understand how much of your success is governed by your team's motivation.
    2. Constantly review your time management.
    3. Become a master of feedback.
    4. Develop your people at every possible opportunity.
    5. Concentrate on managing.
    6. Don't do their job for them; help them to do it themselves.
    7. Understand that you succeed by making others successful.
    8. Work hard at understanding the cultural change that is taking place.
    9. Don't underestimate the power of clarity of purpose on motivation.
    10. Before you decide anything, ask yourself: Is this good or bad for our motivation?
    11. Take yourself seriously.
    12. Understand that the very qualities which made you excel at what you did before becoming a manager are probably precisely the qualities of successful management: listen; create rapport; relate to people; communicate; focus on high leverage points; absorb new ideas and concepts; understand and encourage change; make things happen; accept and master new methods, techniques and skills

**Coming up in this chapter**

> *Getting to know you*
> *Self assessment check up*
> *Building your own motivation*
> *Setting yourself goals and objectives*
> *Spending time on yourself*

## Getting to know you, getting to know all about YOU

Getting to know ourselves and see ourselves 'as others see us' is not always easy. But it is always worth it.

> ❝ *I have incredibly short legs. I used to curse my short legs as a physical flaw. What a waste of my life that period was – once I accepted myself as a short-legged person, my legs were perfect!* ❞
> **– Ron Gilbert offers a lesson on self acceptance**

You are important and special. The fact you are reading this book tells me that you know motivation is important. And you are right. It is increasingly important. So you must include yourself in the motivation building. As I have said before, you will be in no shape to motivate others if you aren't feeling motivated yourself. So we will spend this final chapter looking at how you can power yourself up and face life with permanent positive perkiness!

---

**Self-assessment check up**

This is another exercise you can do on your own, if you so choose; then as you feel it becomes appropriate, do it with your team and discuss their assessment of you. You may already feel quite comfortable about it, in which case use it openly right away. Look at the following list of statements. Score yourself out of 5: if you find you agree entirely with the statement or if it already applies, give yourself 5. If you find you disagree or don't want it to apply, then give yourself 1. Choose anywhere in between to grade yourself.

Be soul-baringly honest. Use this exercise to uncover and help with the planning of your own development. Discuss the results with your own manager and create your personal development plan together.

| | |
|---|---|
| I truly care about my team, and they feel and know it | 1 2 3 4 5 |
| I appraise and assess performance more regularly than other managers | 1 2 3 4 5 |
| I always take feedback after coaching, training and observed activity | 1 2 3 4 5 |
| All our goal setting — as individuals and as a team — is done together | 1 2 3 4 5 |
| My staff respect me and I find this works better than fear and discipline | 1 2 3 4 5 |
| I know my team as individuals and I know how they differ in skills | 1 2 3 4 5 |
| I have looked at motivation on an individual basis and talked about it with each of them | 1 2 3 4 5 |
| I never find that I have to tell them what to do and we talk and work it out together | 1 2 3 4 5 |
| As a team, we always try to make decisions together and this way works better | 1 2 3 4 5 |
| I make a point of knowing the personal needs of my team members | 1 2 3 4 5 |

| | |
|---|---|
| I am always anxious to improve my management skills and my team help me | 1 2 3 4 5 |
| I do not have a problem with my attitude to the company; it's always positive | 1 2 3 4 5 |
| When my team are at their best, they simply have to generate enough acitivity to win | 1 2 3 4 5 |
| My team meetings are interesting, fun, involve the whole team and build motivation | 1 2 3 4 5 |
| The team and I have developed a training plan based on their needs as a unit | 1 2 3 4 5 |
| I feel supported by my manager and know that I can ask for help at any time | 1 2 3 4 5 |
| At team meetings we avoid sarcasm and negativity as they are not helpful | 1 2 3 4 5 |
| Team spirit is something we all value and work at and we like helping each other | 1 2 3 4 5 |
| I am liked and admired by my team | 1 2 3 4 5 |

The maximum score is 95. If you score over 75, apply for a board position now. If you score over 80, check it with your team today. If you score over 85, you have a God-like status. You are also kidding yourself!

## Building your own motivation

Motivating yourself is fairly black and white. If you feel good and positive, you are in a state from which you can motivate yourself. If you feel unhappy or negative, you are not.

Therefore, if there is something making you unhappy at home or at work, you would be well advised to settle it to your satisfaction. If you can only settle it to your dissatisfaction, go ahead and settle it. Then wrap it up and throw it away. Move on to the next happiness in your life.

Here is a step-by-step method to work on your own motivation.

### 1. Decide if you need to work with a friend or colleague

If you do, choose someone you don't mind sharing your innermost feelings with. And choose someone who understands just how important your motivation is to your success. My advice would be to choose someone other than a team member, family member or partner. Let's call this person your counsel.

### 2. Start from your motivation map

It is after all your view of the things you find will motivate you. Reflect again to be sure you have chosen the right scoring.

### 3. Relate back to the Herzberg list of 'hygiene factors' (p. 27)

Check yourself out. Are they all satisfactorily in place for you?

**What if your own hygiene factors aren't there?**

Now you have the same set of choices as the case we considered on page 23. So you are going to have to be firm with yourself. Finding and accepting a satisfactory resolution for yourself is vital and urgent. You are limiting your own personal development, success and growth until your life is content within the first two layers of Maslow's hierarchy of human needs. Don't ever forget – your whole team's motivation is dependent on yours.

### 3. Look at your motivators one by one

Ask yourself – or discuss with your chosen counsel – what positive steps you could take to address each of the topics on your map to increase your motivation

Remember – all of the exercises and advice in the book so far are not just for your team. You can use them for yourself. And, again, if you would benefit from the involvement of a second person, get your counsel to join in. Get them to read this book too!

### 4. Develop an action plan

And pace yourself. Setting achievable goals is an important method of realising your success and recognising your progress

**Setting your goals and objectives**

Here are some ideas to use in setting yourself objectives. Make your goals and objectives SMART*:

**S**pecific
**M**easurable
**A**spirational
**R**ealistic
**T**ime-bound

Make sure you do not suffer from 'objective overload'!

[* When I use or reproduce other people's material I am always anxious to credit them. However, in this case I am not sure where this contribution comes from so whoever it was – thank you!]

**5. Get going!**

And make sure you find ways to nurture yourself. Your work will be less than your best if you don't look after yourself. So many managers excuse themselves from basic niceties or even basic rights that they would never deny their staff. As a manager, you must value, respect and honour yourself. Get enough sleep. Eat sensibly and in tune with your body. Take exercise and stay fit. All of these things are good for you, good for your motivation, good for your career and good for your life.

---

**Old school, new school?**

'Old-school' managers (of whom senior ranks tend still to have quite a few!) may actually feel threatened by much of the material in this book. It's too touchy-feely; too open; too difficult. Empowerment, freedom to think and be creative and devolving responsibility can freak people out. Command and control is what they grew up with – what they know. Change is too difficult – too scary. The older they are or the nearer retirement, the harder it will be for them.

If you should happen to be one of those more mature managers, please grasp the nettle. Why? Because embracing the new is something you can do and be proud of. I have never met anybody yet who hasn't reported that mastering motivation for themselves and others has in any way been anything other than good and positive for their work and personal lives. Whatever 'school' you belong to – old, new or in transition – recognising that the skill of motivation improves your personal life as well as your business life is a breakthrough. You'll develop new friends and strengthen other relationships. You'll be a person people want to be with, want to have with them and want to get to know. Everybody loves a motivator!

---

## Spending time on yourself

Allow yourself the wisdom of spending time on your own motivation. Check yourself out against the list below:

○ *Enthusiasm*
○ *Confidence*
○ *Self-motivation*
○ *Positive attitude*
○ *Energy*
○ *Time management*
○ *Own-time*
○ *Fitness, health and feel-good factors*

What can you do to improve in these areas? How can you grow yourself? Convince your manager that these things are important for you and your own motivation and that he or she should work on this with you. No-one wants a de-motivated manager.

## And finally . . .

Ignore people who tell you that to spend time on yourself is self-indulgent. It is not; it is wise. And it is good for your home and work life. All winners in any sport take excellent care of themselves and keep fit. And so it is with your work. There are no winners of anything who don't use motivation as a major contributor to their success. You can be a winner among motivators. But never forget that the success of your team and their motivation depends on you. So go for it. They deserve it but, just as important, you deserve it.

## And so we say goodbye . . . for now!

As you may have realised, this book is one of a series in which we are covering a combination of the hot topics and old favourites, including direct mail, sales management, building Customer loyalty and now, motivation. Forthcoming are marketing a small business, running meetings, key account management and copywriting. And there will be more. Keep your eyes out for the topics that interest you. And remember, we welcome your stories and experiences via e-mail at jfr@jfr.co.uk. Our website is at www.x-s.co.uk/members/jfr.

Now then, get going! You can be the next Mr Motivator – or the first Ms Motivator!

1. Get to know and accept yourself. Check out your own state using the 'self assessment check-up' exercise. Be completely honest with yourself. Identify your own development needs and discuss them with your manager.

2. Use the five-step checklist to build your own motivation – start from your motivation map; check out your state against the Herzberg hygiene factors; decide the positive steps you can take to improve; create an action plan and set goals that are specific, measurable, aspirational, realistic and time-bound.

3. Spend time on yourself – what can you do to improve your enthusiasm, confidence, self-motivation, positive attitude, energy, time management, own time and fitness, health and feel-good factors?

4. Ignore those who tell you that nurturing yourself and your own needs is self-indulgent. It is not; it is wise.

5. All winners use motivation. Be one of them and remember that your team deserve it but, just as important, you deserve it too.